DAY to DAY

DAY to DAY

Spiritual help when someone you love has Alzheimer's

Cecil Murphey

The Westminster Press
Philadelphia

CONTENTS

ACKNOWLEDGMENTS

I want to express my appreciation to the Atlanta chapter of the Alzheimer's Disease and Related Disorders Association, Inc. (The national address is 70 East Lake Street, Chicago, IL 60601. Upon request they will provide addresses for local chapters.)

Special thanks go to Nancy L. Mace and Peter V. Rabins for their book *The 36-Hour Day* (Baltimore: Johns Hopkins University Press, 1981). Although I do not quote directly from this invaluable publication, I used it as my primary resource.

O N E

First Reactions

"It isn't true . . . is it?"

"It isn't true. . . . It's not—" and I couldn't even name the disease. I heard the doctor's words. I read the reports. I had watched his erratic behavior for months. I still couldn't accept it. Today I catch myself denying it. He isn't that bad, I tell myself. He'll get better. He's tired and confused but he'll pull out of it.

I don't want him sick. I want him like he used to be. But he won't get better. It *is* true, and I can't do anything to prevent the disease's progress. I'm learning—slowly—to accept truths I don't want to know. These days I try to focus on the wonderful memories of our good years together. Suffering Job asked, "Shall we receive good at the hand of God, and shall we not receive evil?" (Job 2:10). And we did have many good years.

Dear God, although I want to deny the reality, give me strength to accept it. Amen.

Groping

Her diagnosis with Alzheimer's threw me into a panic at first. How can I cope? I can't watch her twenty-four hours a day. What if she gets violent? Will I be forced to dump her in a nursing home?

I had a lot of fears and an equal amount of false information. Our doctor sent us to the local ADRDA* chapter. Hearing the people there tell how they coped and what they had to overcome helped. I found people to ask when I ran into problems.

Sometimes I asked and heard ADRDA members say, "I don't know." They offered advice and suggestions but admitted to their own groping in the dark.

God, knowing others have the same kind of problems and anxieties makes it a lot easier. Just to know that I'm not the only one who feels this way gives me peace. Thank you for my wonderful ADRDA group. Amen.

*Alzheimer's Disease and Related Disorders Association. Other conditions have characteristics that are similar to those of Alzheimer's disease. Individuals with these conditions need much the same kind of care as that given to Alzheimer's patients.

Maybe . . . maybe . . .

I've heard the diagnosis. He won't get better. Yet I keep thinking, Maybe the doctors made a mistake. Maybe it's not Alzheimer's. . . .

Other times I speculate, Maybe they'll find a cure soon. Maybe they'll be able to reverse the damage with a medical breakthrough. . . .

Maybe. False hopes. But that's part of me. When the load gets heavy, I find some release this way.

Maybe . . . maybe. . . . I know it won't be, yet as long as he is still alive, I'll keep waiting to hear the doctor's voice on the phone telling me, "We have just made this great discovery. . . ."

God of great expectations, is it foolish for me to hope like this? I love him so much and I don't want to give him up. You understand that, don't you, God?

Why me?

I determined not to feel sorry for myself. I wouldn't give in like those other men I've talked to.

All day I haven't been able to please her no matter what I do. An hour ago she finally calmed down and I'm exhausted. I hear my own inner questions: *Why me? What did I ever do to deserve this kind of punishment? Why do I have to go through all this?*

Then I picked up a scrapbook she kept faithfully through our years together. As I looked I started to remember the good times. Our vacations. The children. Happy moments forever with us both. In the midst of reliving those memories the questions come back: *Why me? What did I ever do to deserve all those happy years?*

When I think of it that way, the problems don't seem quite so heavy anymore.

God, when I ask Why me? *in the sad moments, help me to ask the same question about the happy ones. Amen.*

Healings and cures

I still pray for a miracle. God can do anything, so maybe that includes the healing of damaged brain cells.

I still pray for a medical breakthrough, a new drug that reverses the damage. I hope that some master healer might come along and restore him to the way he used to be.

Some people have traveled to Europe or Asia seeking a cure. They've tried vitamins, pills, special exercises. They have seen no improvement.

I want to be realistic. This is the way it is, I tell myself. Yet deep within me hope remains. Maybe a breakthrough will come. Research is going on at an enormous rate. Each day I still hear myself saying, "What if today . . . ?"

God of all hope, I want a miracle for him—and for me too. I keep asking because part of being alive is to live in hope. Thank you for that. Amen.

Helpless

When we first learned about Mom's illness, we went into a kind of shock. When we learned how she might change, it upset us all. Helplessness and depression hovered over us. And a lot of self-pity. We wanted to do something—anything—and yet we felt overwhelmed by everything.

I remembered an old joke about the way to eat an elephant: one bite at a time. As long as I focused on the total situation and how it affected us, it paralyzed me.

When I shifted thinking and began with the immediate situation, breaking it down into manageable steps, the world didn't look so bleak anymore.

God, we're not helpless. We have you for strength and wisdom. With your help, we know we can cope by taking it one day at a time. Amen.

Why, God?

Why us? Why Dad? Why would God allow this to happen to a good man like him? I start to think of all the bad people in the world who don't have any problems like this—then I stop the cycle because I've been over it a hundred times since we first learned about Dad's illness.

I know I won't find an answer to *Why?* Even if I found an answer, would it satisfy me? Probably not.

Jesus said that the sun and the rain come upon the just and the unjust (see Matt. 4:45). Good people have problems too. I never thought much about that until Dad got sick. Now I think about it often and wish none of us had these problems.

Wise God, I don't understand why life's unfair but I do understand that you're with us. You're also with Dad. Thank you. Amen.

"But she looks fine"

I wonder how often people think she looks fine. They say, "She acts normal," as if they expected to see a slobbering idiot. An old friend said, "She's just being stubborn. That's her whole problem." But I know better. I live with her every day.

Around friends, she behaves well. She covers up her memory loss with a variety of tricks. She changes the subject or says, "I know that!"

It finally dawned on me that she knows something is wrong and it disturbs her. Her immediate defense is, naturally, denial. After talking with her doctor and getting professional help, I can now talk to her about her illness. I frequently assure her, "I love you. I'm always with you, so you don't need to be afraid."

Ever-present God, no matter what, you're with us and you'll never leave us. Help her to know that your loving presence and mine will always be there for her. Amen.

TWO

Facing Alzheimer's Disease

Getting informed

We found a lot of emotional support after we learned about Dad's illness. Our doctor made herself available. We learned about church and governmental programs. We joined an ADRDA support group.

Alzheimer's was only a word until it struck our family. Had we been alert we might have recognized the signs earlier. I suspect that even if we had been alert, we would have denied or overlooked the symptoms. At least that's been typical of the other families we've met.

We've been finding out everything we can through ADRDA. We keep up on the latest research. Hearing of developments, being with others, and sharing insights on how we cope with our individual situations have helped us through the first rough stages.

God, how wonderful that we can learn from each other! Thank you for making it possible to have these sources available. Amen.

"I'm fine"

She began making odd mistakes. She forgot to put beans in the chili. She didn't remember to turn the stove off until the food burned. She took off her glasses and, unable to find them, accused me of hiding them.

Eventually I accepted her accusations as attempts to deny her illness. At first I tried to reason with her, thinking I could help her acknowledge what was wrong. I stopped because I sensed she was not ready or able to admit how sick she was. Instead I comforted her and told her how much I loved her.

One day, with tears in her eyes, she said, "I'm getting worse." It was not a question.

I sensed she had known for a long time that something was wrong. I assured her of my supporting love.

Caring God, all of us are good at denying painful reality. Give us the courage to face unpleasant tasks and to know that you're with us every step of the way. Amen.

"I'm just sad"

Dad lost interest in everything. We couldn't entice him to go anywhere or to do anything. He lost weight and wouldn't eat. When we asked what was wrong, he said, "I'm just sad."

It took a while before we figured out he was depressed. The doctor talked to him and he said, "I'm not right inside. Something's wrong and I'm sad about it." Dad has some awareness of his incurable condition. Not everyone with Alzheimer's does.

We talk more to him. We encourage him to help with things around the house, simple tasks but jobs he can do. He's beginning to come out of his despondency.

God, it saddens us when we see Dad's continuing deterioration. Help us to accept this inevitability and to care for him patiently and lovingly. Amen.

Memory problems

We knew her memory was fading. She stopped remembering names. She lost words when she spoke.

The worst for me came when she constantly talked about her childhood. No matter what anyone said, she'd interrupt and talk about her early days.

At one time I thought she did it deliberately. Now I know differently. I try to listen carefully even though I've heard most of the stories fifty times. I ask simple questions. "Did the sun shine that day? What color dress did you wear?"

We met as adults. Now when she talks about the ancient past, I can almost believe I was with her when the events took place. I feel closer to her.

Eternal God, you brought our lives together. We ask you to help us share all parts of it. Amen.

Feeling lost

He never said he felt lost but I think that's what he meant. He couldn't hold down a job any longer. He didn't have people around to talk to and to do things with. No wonder he felt lost.

He frequently tried to leave the house, having no understanding of where he was going, only that he wanted to get away. Our son installed inside bolts on the door that he couldn't easily release. We hoped they would keep him inside. Yet he continues to go out the door.

A friend advised me to surround him with familiar things, and I've been doing that. He used to collect stamps. I lead him to his favorite chair and lay a stamp album in his lap. He fingers the familiar stamps and it calms him. I think he feels less lost now.

God of the universe, we creatures are so small and easily lost. Yet you never lose sight of us. Remind us that each of us is important to you. Amen.

Limited words

She starts speaking and stops in midsentence. Or the expression on her face tells me she's searching for a word and can't find it.

One woman at our local ADRDA group says that her mother can never complete a full thought. Another reports that her husband's vocabulary seems limited to nouns and verbs like *eat, food, walk*. Others tell of people speaking cyclically by constantly repeating the same word or phrase.

It upsets her when I correct her. I've had to learn to interpret what she wants not only from her words but from her gestures and forty years of knowing her.

Some days I get tired of trying to figure out what she wants but I keep working with it. If the situation were reversed, she'd be as patient with me as she has always been through our years together.

God, when I talk to you I feel inadequate and limited. I wonder, Does she feel that way too? Remind me that our verbal ability has nothing to do with your love for us. Amen.

Losing skills

Before his illness he was so handy he could repair anything. Yet I've been watching him slowly lose his skills. Now it takes effort for him to use a screwdriver.

I tried to keep him at it. "Just try a little harder." It didn't work. Once lost, the skills don't return. I know, and I think he does too.

I select a few of his simple tools and take them to him every day. I hold his hand steady so that he can hammer a nail into a board. Together we take out or put in screws.

Does this accomplish anything? I watch his eyes, and now and then I see a flicker of joy. When that happens, I count it a special day. I believe that although his mind has forgotten his skills, his wizened hands still remember.

Creator God, as we accept losses in life, help us to gain in patience and in understanding. Amen.

Wrong words

"You know I don't like to eat carburetors," she told me. We had been talking about cauliflower. I saw the confused and pained expression on her face even though she didn't understand what she had said.

Nowadays she says a lot of strange things, and often I have to guess at what she's trying to tell me. I know she can't help the way her brain malfunctions. When I start feeling irritated I remind myself of that.

When she uses the wrong word and I can figure out what she means, I act as if she has said it correctly. If I'm not sure, I say, "What? Tell me again." Or, "Please point to it."

While words are important, they are only part of our life together.

God of all languages, remind me that words are symbols, and the person is more important than the words she uses or can't use. Amen.

Rambling

At a restaurant he walked over to a stranger and started talking. The words came fluently enough but he rambled. I felt embarrassed for him and for myself.

It hurt me to see a man I had loved for so many years talking this way. I hurriedly intervened and apologized. Yet I wondered, Did my abruptness hurt him? Since then, I allow him to talk awhile before I touch his arm or say, "We need to move on, dear."

When he rambles he's trying to communicate. While not sure of what he's trying to say, it's his way of fighting and holding on. Instead of contentedly going into a quiet abyss of silence, he's using what verbal facility he has. I want him to talk as much as he can or wants to.

Caring God, we human beings don't always make sense, do we? Yet you never turn away from us. Thank you. Amen.

Lost words

"Pass me that stuff," she said at dinner. Not once did she name anything. I realized then that for a long time she had been concealing the fact that she couldn't think of words when she wanted them.

Most frequently she forgot the common names of things and developed clever ways of talking around them.

When I asked what she meant, she said, "What's the matter? Can't you hear?" Or "I don't want to tell you again. Why do you keep bothering me?" Often she changed the subject.

I sense this problem troubles and confuses her deeply. Often I can guess her meaning. At other times I miss it completely and she lashes out in anger or irritation. But I understand, and it's all right.

Almighty God, sometimes we can't find the words to thank you for being with us. In my case I don't know the words. In her case she can't remember. But we know that you love us both. Amen.

A funny thing

My brother laughed at the way Dad garbled a sentence (but not in Dad's presence). Whenever Dad showed bizarre behavior, he found humor in it.

"How can you be so insensitive?" I asked in shock.

"I love him too, you know," he said. "Sure, his disease is terrible, but what's wrong with seeing a little humor in it? Makes it easier to bear."

I once heard a Peace Corps volunteer say that Africans laugh when a person falls or has an accident. An old man explained, "Laughing is close to crying. We laugh so that we do not cry."

I thought of events from my childhood that seemed so traumatic at the time, but I laugh at them now. "You're right," I told my brother. "We all need a little more laughter in life, don't we?"

God, a little laughter makes the day so much brighter. Help us see the humor and not just the horror of daily events. Amen.

Her defense

Mom doesn't make sense at times. She talks and talks but I can't figure it out. At first I grew impatient and tried to fake a smile to show I was listening. Then I realized that this confused speaking is her only defense. I think Mom suffers because she's aware of her loss of verbal skill. She knows she's slipping.

Since that understanding on my part, I've tried to make it as painless as possible for her. When she can't think of a word, I say "Point to it" or "Describe it." Or I make a game of it: "Let's play twenty questions."

I want Mom to know I can feel her confusion as she goes through this loss of memory. I want her to remain aware that these changes in her don't change us. We love her, no matter how ill she becomes.

God of compassion, as Mom loses her ability with words, help us demonstrate our love without them. Amen.

Independence

He has given up one thing at a time. The ability to shave. Bathing himself. Eating by himself. Each loss may not be significant. As we get older we all lose certain abilities.

But these losses troubled me, and I think they troubled him also, because inability also signals the loss of his independence. He worked hard and provided well for our family. For him to have to depend upon others confuses and troubles him.

Our daughter asked, "Mom, why do we keep talking about his losing his independence? Why not think of it as giving us the opportunity to express our gratitude for all the things he's done for us? Dad was there when we needed him. Now it's our turn."

God, help us to realize that as much as we'd like to do everything for ourselves, sometimes we have to depend on others. Amen.

Falling

She fell three times in one week, and each time it tore me up inside. Fortunately, none of the spills seemed to do any damage.

The first two times I rushed over and started to pick her up. "Just leave me alone!" she screamed. So I watched silently as she slowly pulled herself up, by holding onto the table the first time, and the door the second.

On her third fall, I sat down on the floor next to her and checked to make sure she had not injured herself. I patted her hand and we sat in silence.

The verse "Though he fall he shall not be utterly cast down" (Ps. 37:4) helped me ponder the number of times I've failed God. Yet God is always there to pick me up—if I ask. After a few minutes I got up and then bent down and helped her to stand.

God my protector, thank you for picking me up when I fall. And thank you for doing it gently. Amen.

Not the same

He's not the same man I married. No matter how much I tell myself he is, a part of me won't listen.

I loved the way he laughed over simple, silly things. He doesn't laugh anymore. I loved the way his eyes twinkled when I did something that pleased him. He doesn't even smile very much now. I loved his strength and felt safe just being with him. Sometimes he doesn't even know who I am.

He's not the same. He'll never be the same. Yet I can call on my memories. I think of his gentle touch, his self-conscious smile. The way he said my name like nobody else. The feel of his body next to mine.

He'll never be the same, I know that. Yet sometimes . . . sometimes I wish it were different.

God, I wish I could choose how our two lives would end. I don't understand why he can't be the same. But I know that you're with him just as much as you're with me. Amen.

Suspicions

"She's trying to steal my savings and put me in a home," Mother told her minister. A wise man, he replied warmly, assuring her of his loving concern.

It hurt me to hear that accusation. I try to give her the best care and I'm not interested in any financial benefit. She's my *mother*.

I'm learning that suspicions come out as part of her illness. While they're not true and she's unaware of her impairment, sometimes I get over-tired or depressed. Then I wonder if, deep within her heart, she thinks I'm trying to take advantage of her. I want her to know I love her and wouldn't do anything to hurt her.

God, it hurts when Mother misinterprets. I'm more so-phisticated but I have a lot of uncertainties in my life, too. Reassure me of the security in your love as I try to show Mother my love. Amen.

Inconsistent

Yesterday he brushed his teeth. Today he stared at the toothbrush as if to ask, What is this?

One day he does a task but not the next. Later he's able to do it again. Having a brain disease causes natural fluctuations.

I now break tasks down into small step-by-step procedures. I get out both toothbrushes and put on paste while he watches. I hand him a brush and he imitates me. If he still has difficulty, I guide his brush into his mouth, and beginning the brushing action often triggers his action.

In many ways I demonstrate and he imitates. Usually he understands because I use familiar objects and actions. Beginning the motions helps the brain remember how to do them. When he can't do a task I try to accept it. But when he does it easily I make that a joyful occasion. I know he's trying.

Dear God, his inconsistencies still irritate me. Yet when I realize that all of us, even at our best, are inconsistent, it makes me more understanding. Amen.

She drinks

We knew Mother drank but we didn't realize that it aggravated her dementia. Her doctor urged her to stop. Out of concern, we hounded her about the amount she drank. Then we learned that it was not the amount but the result that mattered.

We finally cut off her liquor supply and we never faced anything so difficult. She argued, complained, demanded, threatened. She accused us of stealing from her and of hating her. But we held firm for her own good.

More than once I felt like shouting, Give it to her! Anything is better than all this yelling.

We believe we have slowed down the progress of her disease. She's now eating better and we're glad we held out.

God, even when you do things for our own good, we don't always like it. Help us learn that your doing things for us isn't always easy or pleasant for us to accept. Amen.

Shakes and tremors

When our son offered to take him for a ride, he tried to put on his shoes by himself. His hands started shaking. Angrily he threw the shoe across the room. He was nervous about going out with our son instead of with just me.

When anyone comes into the house, he's more apt to shake or show clumsy action. Occasionally he starts walking across the room and stops. He is unable to walk farther unless someone diverts his attention or helps him move.

When he begins to shake or behave awkwardly I smile at him and guide his hand to complete the action by himself. When he starts to shake or tremble, I hold his hand momentarily. "Dear, it's all right, it doesn't matter." Because it doesn't.

God, I've wavered in my devotion to you and yet you always steady me. Help me to offer him the same kind of steadying hand that you hold out to me. Amen.

Once upon a time

The other day I walked out of the room and returned in less than a minute. She looked at me accusingly and said, "Where have you been? I've been waiting hours for you to come back."

I don't argue because her sense of time is gone. For her to understand how much time has passed means she must also remember what she did in the immediate past. She can't do that because she can't recall the immediate past and has no concept of time.

Occasionally she worries about time. When she keeps asking, I sense an anxiety in her. I answer, but I also give her personal attention and affection. I want to eliminate as much anxiety as possible. When I sit and relax with her or hold her hand, she acts less concerned.

God, time and eternity are the same to you. Help me remember that time is not the most important thing in the world. Amen.

Sundowning

I had never heard of sundowning before we joined ADRDA. It refers to the behavior problems that develop in the late afternoons or evenings.

My husband shows this response. He gets more agitated and paces a lot after it gets dark.

We tried different approaches to make him more restful, such as cutting out evening activities. I no longer watch television at night. We asked friends and relatives to make calls and visits earlier in the day.

I watch for other things that upset him so we can avoid them as much as possible. I used to sew in the evenings, but it bothered him; I don't know why. Now I sew after he's asleep. Making things easier for him lightens the load for me.

God, we all have our peak hours and our low moments each day. Keep me responsive to his moods and needs. Amen.

Already lost

I watched her walk across the room this morning and she looked the same as ever. A little older, grayer, slower, but still the same.

Yet I've already lost her. Her body is here. Sometimes she talks. Often she doesn't make sense or she rambles. I've lost her already and yet she's still here. I never dreamed it would cause me so much pain.

If a severe physical illness confined her to bed, would that make it easier? I don't know.

I wish I could reason with her. I wish we could have those long talks the way we used to. I try to tell myself we're still communicating. Then I see the blankness in her eyes and I know she's already lost to me. And it hurts.

God of all comfort, telling you about my pain helps. Thanks for understanding what I often can't open up and tell others. Amen.

THREE

Adapting
to
Alzheimer's
Disease

Structured freedom

How much routine do I establish? How much choice do I offer? I decided that I would be as flexible as possible except to have set times for meals, medication, exercise, and bedtime. I try to do things in the same way each day.

I keep the furniture in the same place even though I'd like to move it occasionally. I don't leave magazines, papers, or clutter around. I want to keep things as simple and easy as possible for him.

When it's time for our daily walk, I tell him what we're going to do. I put on my walking shoes while he watches. Then I put his shoes on. When we're ready to go, I take his hand and we go out the front door—the only time we use that door. Aside from these established routines, I allow him freedom during the rest of the day.

Creator God, you gave us seasons and times and yet freedom within those structures. Help me to provide both freedom and routine for him. Amen.

Change

I couldn't take it anymore. I couldn't plan anything because I never knew from one hour to the next how she was going to react. I had no control. Her erratic behavior kept our lives in continuous chaos.

One day the bath took only twenty minutes but the next day it took two hours. On Thursday she sat quietly most of the day watching TV. Friday she paced the house, bumping into things, talking constantly, and I couldn't understand what she was saying.

A friend suggested that I find one or two things that I could change and control. I did that. For example, instead of having friends just drop in, I worked out a schedule so I could leave the house for an hour three afternoons a week. That simple change made a big difference. I'm in control of at least one thing and I don't feel so trapped by circumstances.

All-powerful God, guide me to know where I can still make choices. Amen.

Day to day

At first I worried about the future and what lay
ahead for him. I cried a lot through that difficult
period. If it's this bad now, what's it going to be
like in the days ahead? I thought. How can I
possibly cope?

Before his illness, cooking a meal didn't take
much effort. Now, because of his constant need
for care and attention, cooking takes hours longer
with his interruptions. I don't mind dressing him,
but all the struggling with him takes so much out
of me.

I decided I had to stop worrying about the
future and to take life with him on a day-to-day
basis. Each morning I pray for strength for just
this day. I frequently remind myself of the words
of Jesus: "Do not worry about tomorrow, for
tomorrow will worry about itself" (Matt. 6:34,
NIV).

*Eternal God, help me cope with today's problems today.
Amen.*

Learning new things

I refused to accept the reality that she could not learn new things. Simple things like finding the way out of a store or returning to where we parked the car. "We're leaving the car in the yellow zone," I said. She didn't remember. I tried to stimulate her thinking or to trick her into recalling. Nothing worked.

Finally I admitted the truth. However, I taught her simple tasks. When the mail arrives, we go outside together and collect it. I hand everything to her. Although she moves clumsily, she can use a letter opener and take out the folded sheets.

It took weeks for her to master that task but now it's her primary daily job. Some days she rewards me with a smile, and I like to think she's saying, Thanks, for letting me do this one thing.

Giver of all life and skills, help me to learn better so that I can be a better teacher. Amen.

Adapting

I'm methodical and I like to schedule things. I once washed on Monday, cleaned house on Thursday, and saved Friday for shopping. I've had difficulty adjusting to this new phase of our lives.

I accept that I can't plan like that anymore. What used to be normal no longer has relevance. I have adapted to the way he is instead of trying to do things "the right way."

Sometimes he wants to sleep with his hat on. He wears gloves in the tub. He can't manage a spoon or fork so I let him use his fingers and serve finger foods as much as possible. It's easier to let him do those things than to argue. It makes him happier and I stay calmer.

I've given up doing things the way we used to. I've tried to use common sense and a little imagination in adapting. It makes life easier for both of us.

All-wise God, give me wisdom to adapt lovingly. Amen.

Calming techniques

No matter how hard I tried I became upset. I demanded of her what she could no longer do.

Now when I get frustrated, I stop, breathe deeply a few times, and force myself to speak gently. I talk about one topic at a time, keep it simple and easy for her to grasp. I walk slowly and quietly. When she starts to get agitated, holding her hand seems to have a calming effect.

Sometimes it helps when I stand behind, with my arms around her, and gently rock her. Playing soft, slow, familiar songs on the record player soothes her. Since the ringing telephone jars her, I keep it on low. We have a note on the front door asking people to knock rather than ring the bell. I'm learning new ways to help her remain calm. Or perhaps these are techniques that help me to stay calm.

God of peace, thank you for teaching me to be calm. Amen.

A world of suggestions

My sister took care of Dad for six months and she couldn't handle him anymore. "Now it's your turn," she said.

Caring for Dad meant a long period of adjustment for both of us. My sister called every day, loading me down with advice. My brother, who has never taken care of him, phones weekly with new bits of wisdom. He doesn't know the strain of living with Dad every day, twenty-four hours each day.

As soon as I tell people he has Alzheimer's, they tell me about a person they knew and how the family handled it. "No two people are the same," I answer, but I don't think they hear me. They're positive they know what to do.

I constantly fought resentment. Then a friend said, "They want to help. Accept the advice as they intend it, not as the way it doesn't work." I'm thankful for *that* suggestion!

God, thanks for those who want to help. Help me receive advice as loving gifts. Amen.

Rush and hurry

I've always been in a hurry to get things done, but I had to learn a whole new way of life in giving care to my wife. I can't rush her. When I try, I confuse or disturb her. It took me awhile to admit that she wasn't deliberately slowing me down. She couldn't help it.

One day I became so frustrated because it was taking so long to get anything done with her, I remember praying for help: Immediately the idea came to me. Time is a friend to enjoy, not an enemy to conquer.

I relaxed. I looked into those vacant eyes and said to my wife, "I'm sorry, dear. I don't have to hurry and rush, I have all the time I need."

Even more important, the time I have is with her—the most important person in my life.

Patient God, remind me to slow down and to cultivate friendship with time. Amen.

Appointment rushing

Two days ago I caught myself rushing him so that we could reach the doctor's office by ten thirty. In my rushing, I dropped a spoon and knocked over the orange juice. When I became aware, I slowed down. "We have to go to the doctor this morning," I said, "and we may be a little late, but we'll get there."

I also saw that my rushing had made him nervous. I sat down next to him and held his hand. By the time he had quieted, I had also calmed down.

We arrived ten minutes late for the appointment, but I walked in with a peaceful husband. The rest of my day went more smoothly too.

Maker of time, remind me that life is smoother when I go calmly about my tasks. Amen.

Household safety

She left the iron on, and it could have caused a fire. Another time she didn't turn off the water tap, and it overflowed the basin. I'm learning to watch these things carefully.

I make sure she won't trip over furniture. I no longer stack anything on the stairs. I lowered the temperature on our water heater so that when she does turn on the tap, she won't scald herself. I removed the medicine from the bathroom because she tried to take additional amounts. I keep it in a locked closet.

I put away her beautiful antique glassware, moved furniture with sharp edges, and eliminated throw rugs. I removed door locks from the bathroom and bedroom. I've gone through the house with two thoughts in mind: utility and safety. Her safety is more important than what we own.

God, keep our home safe and help me to make it safe for her. Amen.

Outdoor safety

He used to love to garden and rake leaves in the fall. He can't do that now. I've given away his tools for his own safety. I can't even let him walk around in the backyard alone. One day he tripped on the uneven ground and fell.

Another time he lost his balance going down the three steps on the back porch. Since then we have installed a handrail, painted bright red. Our storm doors now have iron grilles so he can't put his arm through and cut himself.

The hardest for me has been his daily walk with the dog. He couldn't do it alone any longer, and he resented my going along with him. We gave the dog away. Now he walks with me around the block every day. For a while, with one activity after another, it depressed me to think, He'll never be able to do this again. Instead of that negativity I remind myself that I am making life easier for him.

God of all comfort, give us both peace as we make these necessary adjustments. Amen.

The better driver

We both knew she was the better driver. On trips I let her take the wheel. I can't do that any longer. Her reactions are too slow. When anything unusual happens in traffic she gets confused. She can't make decisions easily. I kept putting off asking her to stop driving, not wanting to take away this pleasure. I finally knew I had to when she caused a minor accident that should never have happened.

A friend advised, "Don't blame her and don't put her down." The next time we went out, I said, "Why don't you watch the scenery today and I'll drive?" She nodded her agreement.

She's said nothing about driving again. I like to think it relieved her. I also like to think she understands that while she was the better driver, I have to do it now.

God, as we realize that she can't do things she once did, remind us that you're there to help us. Amen.

Car loss

He'll never drive a car again. He's taken such good care of our cars. More than just not being able to drive, giving it up symbolizes a lot of things he'll never do again.

He was a skilled driver, moving effortlessly through crowded lanes while he talked or listened to the radio. A few months ago I saw how upset he became when he had to drive in heavy traffic. He forgot a turn and a car almost hit us. Fortunately he made the transition easy for me. "You'd better drive," he said, trying to sound casual. "Downtown traffic gets on my nerves."

He tried to smile, but I know what it cost him to turn the driving over to me. Other wives have had trouble making the change. They took over when they realized that it involved human safety—theirs and others.

God, give both of us strength to accept what we can't change. Amen.

Remembering

Mother's older sister, Mary, lives out of state but visits a week at a time. It gives me more free time, and it does something for Mother, too.

They talk about their childhood. They relive the pranks they pulled, the fun they had, even the redheaded boy they fought over.

Mary asks, "Do you remember the time—?" It surprised me how much Mother recalled. I'm doing that now, too. We talk about the things Mother taught me. We remember family vacations. We giggle over my teenage worries about acne and dates.

The remembering perks her up. I've also realized something else—I get a lift too.

God of all eternity, thank you for the good times in our past. Thank you that we can remember and, in small measure, relive them. Amen.

FOUR

Living with Alzheimer's Disease

Sharing concerns

We used to talk things out before his illness. Since then I have felt totally alone. I make decisions for him. That was bad enough, but it got worse when he refused to cooperate.

He didn't want a bath. He refused to take his medication. He cried when I made him go to bed.

I started talking quietly, sharing my frustrations. Did he understand my words? The tone of my voice? I don't know, but he calmed down. Since then, when he gets difficult, I say, "Honey, I don't like what's happening either. I get frustrated too." When I take time to share my problems, he usually calms down and it's easier for both of us.

Understanding God, help me to remember that he is with me to share my life. I want him to share in working through the problems too. Amen.

Talking to

Some days it seems as if she has no idea what goes on. Visitors come and because she doesn't respond, they talk about her as if she weren't present. "Talk directly to her," I say. "She's right here."

We've shared many years together, and I want her to remain part of my life for as long as possible. I speak to her much as I used to, although I have had to learn to speak more calmly. I tell her what we're going to do and why. I ask her, "Dear, would you like to have your bath now or would you like to watch TV?" When I have decisions to make, I sit beside her with my arm around her shoulder and explain the situation. Just talking aloud to her helps. I like to think that she knows I consult her on everything—the way I've always done.

God, I don't usually hear you speak, yet I know you're present. Help me to remember her presence too. Amen.

Simplifying

I dreaded helping him get dressed in the morning because he couldn't manage the buttons. He refused my help and ended up tearing his shirt.

I finally bought him shirts without buttons. We turned to loafer-type shoes. I put elastic in his trousers and sewed the zippers shut. I also bought jogging pants. As he loses his dexterity, I search for ways to simplify each activity. When I realize a problem is coming up, I search for ways to simplify the task so that he can still do as much for himself as possible.

The other day he simplified the problem of taking his pills. I had been giving them to him one at a time, pausing for him to wash it down with milk or juice. He dumped all the pills into the glass, drank it down in a single swallow, and laughed when he did it. I thanked him for helping me solve that one.

All-loving One, thank you that we can enjoy the simple moments together. Amen.

Affection

I heard that everybody needs four hugs a day for survival, eight for maintenance, and twelve for growth.*

I think of that when she wants to communicate with me and can't. At least I want her to know I love her, that I'm with her and not going to leave.

I hold her a lot. When she does anything right, I hug her. I hug her when she's frustrated, or stroke her cheek. Many times we sit close together, our bodies touching.

I look for ways to kiss her that she enjoys, such as on the ears or the tip of her nose, then give her a bright smile. She always returns the smile.

God, at times I feel as if you were wrapping your arms around me, and I understand your concern for me. Help me to communicate my affection and concern for her in the same way. Amen.

---

*Attributed to Virginia Satir.

Exercised bodies

He didn't want to do anything except sit or pace the room. He didn't sleep well at night, and that disturbed my rest.

Then I hit upon an exercise program. The local shopping mall opens its doors two hours early for the sick and recuperating to walk in the air-conditioned atmosphere. We have been doing this for months. Some days he smiles or laughs at things we see in the windows. He likes the bright colors. We never see more than twenty people the whole time we're there, and that makes it easier for him too.

I like to think this daily exercise slows down his disease. He sleeps more soundly now, usually without awakening all night. This morning, I kept thinking of all the movements we can make. What an incredible God we have who provides us with such a remarkable body!

Creator God, when you made our bodies you did a wonderful job. Help us to care for them. Amen.

Meaningful movements

One day I picked up a pile of old records we used to dance to. I put on one of the records and immediately felt sorry about her restricted physical activities. To my amazement, she came over and held out her arms for a dance.

Since then we dance together nearly every day in our living room, in a space of twenty feet by ten. This fun time has become our exercise program. Others go to senior citizens' exercise classes. Some walk. We have found an exercise that gives us both pleasure.

Yesterday I played, "The Waltz You Saved for Me." She looked into my eyes and kissed my cheek. That made it a special day for me—and I hope for her as well.

Loving God, thank you for the little joys of life, especially for those special moments of togetherness with the ones we love. Amen.

That **habit**

"Someone's knocking at the door," he said and got up to answer. No one was there. No one was ever there.

I kept telling myself I would get used to it. But I didn't. It happened again and again.

I took him to the door and opened it. I tried to reason. I argued. He'd say, "All right," yet within an hour he'd say again, "Someone's knocking."

I gritted my teeth, I counted to ten. I·walked out of the room. That one habit was driving me crazy.

Then I tried a new approach. I ignored the statement. I held him or showed him affection. He still insists someone is at the door, but not quite as often. Then I wondered, Is he trying to invite me to come into his world? Does "hearing" the knock express his need?

God, at times I feel alone, confused, abandoned by everyone. Like him, I also need assurance of your love and your presence. Amen.

Personal care

She stopped taking baths and wore the same dress for days. "Honey, you've already worn that a week," I said. "I put it on clean this morning," she replied angrily.

Since then I put her dirty clothing away at night. Before she gets up in the morning I pick out each item for her to wear. That has helped us to avoid the arguments. As she gets worse I know that her personal care will demand more of me. Yet I don't worry a lot about the future. I concentrate on doing the best I can each day.

I want her to look and feel her best. Instead of these being difficult times for us, I try to make them quiet times of togetherness.

I hope the care I give her body helps her grasp how much I love her.

Heavenly Father, may I be as mindful of her personal needs as you are of mine. Amen.

Sharing

We had a ritual at the end of the day. We sat on the sofa, held hands, and shared our activities with each other.

When I stayed home raising children, it meant a great deal to me to hear about the outside world. Later, when I went to work, we loved comparing our days and laughing over the little things.

I miss the sharing of the little things. I still try. I make us both a cup of tea and we sit, hand in hand, on the same sofa. I tell him the events of my day. It's not the same—it can never be the same—but it's important to me. I don't know if he understands anything. But he still sits beside me, and I know he would share his day with me if he could remember it.

I cried a lot over his memory impairment. We had many, many good times of sharing together. Yet, in our limited way, we're still sharing.

God, thank you that we shared so much. No matter what happens, I still have the memories. Amen.

She or it?

The anger built up, but I felt helpless to do anything about it.

Strangely enough, Mother herself helped me put the situation into perspective. She asked, "Why are you mad at me?"

"I'm not mad at you," I said. That's when I understood. Mom can't help being sick. She's not being stubborn or mean. She's suffering.

I learned to separate Mother from her sickness. I can lash out in anger because of what *it* does to her. I hate the situation that exists. I hate it because I can't do anything to cure her. I'm angry because I'm helpless to fix the confusion of her mind.

But I can truthfully say, "Mom, I'm not mad at you." I don't want her this way. I want the mother I used to know. But she's not available to me anymore.

God, I get angry at the disease and its effects on Mom. Help me to remember I'm angry at it *and not at her. Amen.*

Dollars and sense

At the checkout counter he handed the cashier a five-dollar bill and pulled change out of his pocket. He stared blankly at the coins for a moment and started handing them to her.

"Sir, I only need thirty-seven cents." He had given her three quarters. This was no isolated incident. For weeks he had been confused about money—particularly in making change or counting bills in his wallet.

I tried to be careful in the way I talked about money. I wanted him to feel secure in having cash with him even though he had lost the concept of its worth. I put three one-dollar bills in his wallet and pennies and nickels in his pockets. This satisfied him.

God, even though he has lost the ability to distinguish between dollars and cents, give me wisdom and common sense in living with this situation. Amen.

Paying the bills

Mother always paid her bills by check. As her dementia increased she continued to try to pay the bills, but she made the checks unreadable or put in wrong figures.

Being accountable for money has always been important to Mom, and I don't want to take that away. Yet she frustrates me when she insists on handling her money. Once she accused me of stealing from her.

I suggested, "Why don't I take over paying the bills?"

"You don't trust me, is that it?"

I waited a few days and handed her a book of blank checks and let her work on them. After she went to sleep I wrote the checks properly. Usually we handle this satisfactorily. When Mom gets difficult I remember that because she's conscientious she wants to hold on to this task, and perhaps her dignity as well.

God, thanks for a mother faithful in her duties. Give me patient wisdom in living with her. Amen.

Looking ahead

He's sick, and it takes so much out of me to care for him. Jesus told us not to fret about tomorrow, but I can't help it. If it's this bad now, what will it be in six months? A year? As he gets worse, what will I do?

I get concerned about my inability to care for him. Many nights I go to bed feeling so tired I wonder if I will get up the next morning. Yet I always do. I have to. But can I keep going? What if my health fails? Unpleasant as it is, I can't help thinking about what I'll do when the situation gets worse.

All-caring God, I couldn't cope now if I didn't have you to talk to. On days like today when I'm so tired, I find peace by reminding myself of your promise, "And as your days, so shall your strength be."* Thank you for giving me that to rest upon. Amen.

---

*Deuteronomy 33:25.

Trapped

I feel trapped. Mother needs me. We've never been close. I called her manipulative. She called me calculating. She always acted jealous over the attention Dad showed me.

Now she's sick. When I first realized that I had to take care of her, I resented her. I resented her sickness. I hated God for doing this to me.

I've slowly changed. I still have a lot of bad moments. Old resentments flare up. I'm learning to love my mother. She depends on me, and I have a chance to be the loving "parent" I accused her of not being. It's my turn and it's not easy. I can understand a little of what she must have gone through with me.

God, instead of being trapped, help me to feel you've given me a second chance to build a loving relationship with the mother I never understood. Amen.

Giving up

One day I cried for a long time because I realized all the things that he will never do again. The more I thought, the more things came to mind.

He'll never drive again. He'll never set up the barbecue grill. He'll never waltz with me again. Nor will he ever again usher at our church and take up the offering.

Then I wiped my eyes and said, "But he's still alive. He can still do some things. Even if he couldn't do anything for himself, he's still here and we're still together. He is still somebody— somebody I love."

That sad day when I cried so long helped me remember that he's much more than the things he did. He's more important than anything he has to give up.

God, you gave up your only Son for us. That tells me you endowed us with life. Thanks for helping me understand that who we are means more than what we can or can't do. Amen.

"I feel so guilty"

All my life I've felt guilty. A lot of it I blamed on Mother and told her so many times.

After her surgery we brought her to our home to recuperate. Physically she got better, but her behavior was strange. That's when we found out she had Alzheimer's. Then I worried. Did I help bring it on? If I had been a better child, would she be different today?

As her condition worsened, we talked about a nursing home. I felt fresh guilt about "putting her away." I also felt guilty for the disruption she causes in our home.

Joining a local ADRDA group and hearing others say some of the same words has helped. I still feel guilty. Maybe I'll always feel that way. But I'm learning to make decisions about her welfare—and that of my family—despite the guilt.

God, I wish I didn't feel guilty, but I do. Help me to do what's best for her and for us, despite the nagging doubts and questions. Amen.

"I'm worried"

I hate to hear the well-meant advice, "Don't worry." I can't unplug my concern like a toaster. I constantly give in to fears, worries, anxieties, wondering what would happen if . . .

Some days I get over the worries easily enough by saying, "I can do nothing about it. What will be will be."

The worst times come when I go to bed and can't sleep. What will he do if I become sick? What if he needs a lengthy hospitalization and our money runs out? To help me overcome worry when I try to sleep, a friend printed and framed for me the words of Psalm 4:8: "In peace I will both lie down and sleep; for you alone, O LORD, makest me dwell in safety."

Many nights I lie in bed and read them fifty times before I finally drift into a peaceful sleep.

God, you're always available when I call. I forget that so often. Help me remember. Amen.

"I'm a sexual person"

I never thought I'd talk about sex and especially about *my* sexual needs, but I finally did in an ADRDA support group. I did it more out of desperation than in expectation of their help.

"I'm a sexual person," I said. "I miss it. She's lost all interest, and I don't want to rape her."

They understood. Some of them have had the same kinds of needs. Hearing them talk about their own dilemmas helped me. Then someone said, "I miss the touching, the physical contact, more than the act itself." That insight helped me immensely. Since then I give her more affection. I hold her. I kiss her on the cheek. A few times she has responded by kissing me. Her hand in mine makes me feel better.

God, I am a sexual being, and so are all your creatures. Help me in coping with my needs as I realize they're normal and part of being human. Amen.

"If only . . ."

"For of all sad words of tongue or pen, the saddest are these: 'It might have been!' "*

Those words remind me of the missed opportunities in both our lives. The times I wanted to say, "Dad, I love you," but I didn't. Moments when I might have listened. Incidents where I could have followed his advice. What would our relationship be like if I had been more thoughtful and less critical? It doesn't help to say, "If only I had. . . ."

Intellectually I know that. Emotionally, I wish I could redo a lot of things. Now that Dad's sick I want to do whatever I can for him. Later I want to look back and say, "I did my best. I have no regrets."

God, since I can't change the past, help me make the present as loving and as kind for Dad as I can. Amen.

---

*John Greenleaf Whittier, "Maud Muller."

What about me?

We've known for months that Mother has Alzheimer's. Knowing the name has helped us in coping with her illness. She's not easy to care for, but we'll manage. My family is supportive of me and of her. But that's not what troubles me most right now. Will I have Alzheimer's too? Will my children have to care for me as I care for her? *Don't let this happen to me, dear God, please don't let this happen to me!*

I've asked doctors and members of our ADRDA group. They have no evidence that anyone can inherit Alzheimer's. They do say there is a slightly higher chance that the offspring of an Alzheimer's patient will develop the disease than for the rest of the population.

I have found help in repeating one of the mottoes of Alcoholics Anonymous: "One day at a time." Right now I need to concentrate on today. Just today.

God, keep me peaceful as I remind myself that you're in control of the world and in control of all of my life. Amen.

Only me

I woke up tired today and wished I could spend the morning in bed. I can't. He'll be stirring soon, and I have to care for him the rest of the day. I wish others would help more. Just come in for a couple of hours to talk with him. Take him for a ride. But there's only me.

Church friends have said, "If you need anything, please call." Maybe they mean it. But I keep thinking, Can't you see that I need help? Why don't you just volunteer? Why do I have to be the only one?

No matter how much the others help or want to relieve me, I'm still the only one who thinks of him twenty-four hours a day. Even when I have time away from him I worry. No one can do for him what I can. Maybe that's why I'm the only one.

Dear God, remind me that you're with me. I'm not his only caregiver. Amen.

Only one of me

On a lot of days I wish I were two people. Caring for Mother drains me of energy and I feel I cheat my own children. "I may be a good daughter but I'm a terrible parent," I said.

I can't neglect her, and I don't want to do less for the children. One day I think I've got it figured out, and the next day I'm as confused as ever. Some days if I can just keep the energy flowing until bedtime I feel it's an accomplishment.

When will it end? I don't know, and who can ever say? Maybe I'll always feel this tug between her and the children—it comes from me, not from them. It's my problem to resolve.

God, in times like this I'm confused and don't know what to do or how to spread my time and energy. Give me daily wisdom. Amen.

Other lives, other people

On TV a man walked down the street, talking to the woman he loved. As I watched the scene, my eyes filled with tears. That man's distinctive walk triggered memories of the way my husband used to be.

When I think of friends, sometimes I resent their health and vitality. I don't want life to be like this for him. I want us to be like other people. But we're not other people. He has Alzheimer's.

Then I wonder about the problems of those people I envy. Are our troubles just more obvious? Are theirs deeply hidden? Are they as carefree as the other lives I see on TV? Or does it just look that way because of our particular problems?

Dear God, I fight resentment when I see so much health and youth around me. Please help me to accept the problems I have and not to compare our lives with others. Amen.

Seeing

I wore a Kelly green tie with a royal blue suit. I couldn't tell that the two colors clashed, so she had to tell me. After that I depended on her to let me know what looked good together.

I can't depend on her doing that anymore. She can no longer distinguish easily between colors, particularly pastels. Worse, sometimes she bumps into the walls or furniture because of failing eyesight.

I keep telling her, "My eyes aren't perfect, but they're still pretty good. I'll become the eyes for both of us." Once in a while I jokingly say, "Think of me as your two-legged Seeing Eye dog." It's hard on her, losing her vision, and it hurts me to know she can't embroider now or do hundreds of other little things. But she is alive, and that's the most important thing.

All-seeing God, I don't understand why she is losing her vision. Help me to see for us both. Amen.

All our friends

We used to have a lot of friends and involved ourselves in a variety of social activities. Within months of his diagnosis, those friends drifted away. Some of the relationships lapsed because I didn't have the energy to keep them up.

For a while I felt angry, hurt, rejected, unwanted and unloved. Then I decided I could choose to feel sorry about the situation or make changes.

Our church has a senior citizens' group. We joined the local chapter of ADRDA. I ask our children to come over occasionally and stay with him while I go out. I contacted a few of our former friends and said, "I need help. Just phone him or come by now and then." They responded to my plea.

Our circle of friendship is more limited than before, but I think of it as more select.

God of love, your friendship sustains me in the hard moments. Your friendship to us through others gives new hope and enjoyment in life. Amen.

Selfishness

I used to catch myself wanting to forget she's sick. I fantasized walking out of the house, not caring where I went or how long I stayed away. Then I felt selfish.

I miss going to ball games. I gave up my duties at church. I don't drink coffee with my old pals anymore. I fantasized doing those activities again. Then I felt selfish.

Yet I've recognized now that it's all right for me to miss activities I enjoyed in the past. As long as she needs me I'll be right here with her. No matter how much I'd like life to be different, this is the way it is.

On days when she's at her worst, my fantasy journeys keep me going. They provide places of refuge from the constant problems I face. So I've decided it's all right to think selfish thoughts now and then.

Giving God, thank you for allowing me to have my selfish moments. Amen.

Regrets

We planned that one day we would travel together for at least six months. We'll never do that now. That's one big regret.

I have regrets about the way I treated him in the beginning of his illness. I didn't know he was sick. Neither did he. I wonder now if he wasn't as frightened as I was.

I think of the plans we'll never fulfill. Sometimes the mistakes of the past trouble me. I find myself saying, "If only I had. . . ."

Then I remind myself that if I spend my energy and time in regretting the past, I'll have no time for living now. No time for giving him the care and the love he needs. I'm learning I can live with what I can't change. Yet once in a while, a few regrets pop out.

Mighty God, erase my regrets. Teach me thankfulness for what I have now. Amen.

Doing enough?

Am I doing enough for her? When I asked a friend, he laughed. "You're with her all the time. You never go anywhere. You care for her every minute of the day and sometimes half the night." Yet I keep wanting to do more. To make her comfortable. To hold back the disease's progress. To keep the atmosphere pleasant.

"What else could you do?" he asked. I didn't know. Yet I constantly have this vague ache inside that I could do something beyond what I'm presently doing.

I've come to believe mine is a natural reaction. I can't give her back anything she's lost. I can't make her young or restore her memory.

I also have to face my own limitations. I can't cure her or make her better or take away her confusion. But I can be with her and care for her.

Ever-present God, let me draw from your strength as I give her my best. Amen.

Natural negatives

I have to remind myself that he can't help it when he doesn't cooperate. He can't remember how to do things. Yet once in a while I get frustrated and angry. I want him to do things for himself.

Some days I'm angry at him for being sick. I resent giving up my life to be his caregiver. Some days I hate the whole world.

For a while I told myself I shouldn't be angry. If I truly loved him I wouldn't feel resentment. Good people serve without complaining.

Margie, in our ADRDA support group, helped me when she said, "I love meeting with you all. I can tell you about the terrible feelings I have and you understand." That's right, I thought, I'm only human. I have perfectly natural emotions. I'm not a bad person for feeling as I do.

God of all emotions, help me to accept my natural negatives. Amen.

Forgiving our feelings

She's sick and can't help it. It's not her fault. Not anybody's fault. Just one of those things that happens.

But my feelings didn't cooperate with my mind yesterday. *Why did she do this to me? This isn't fair! Why did she make me have to look after her?*

Then I felt ashamed of my feelings. I finally told a friend. He said, "We all get like that sometimes. You can't help what you feel. After all, you're not quite perfect yet." Then he said, "I hope you'll forgive your feelings. Anger is just one way of showing your hurt and your confusion. Life isn't fair to any of us. Yet most of us get a lot more good out of it than we deserve."

God, when I feel angry, hurt, or resentful, help me to accept those feelings and to forgive myself. I'm human, and I live with human emotions. Amen.

Nobody knows

I feel so alone. He demands all my time and my strength. I'm not complaining about that, because I married him and I'll stick with him "for better for worse." I know he'd do the same for me.

But I feel no one else understands what I'm going through. Even the children aren't here enough to see the drain, the demand, the isolation.

Today on the radio I heard a spiritual that I haven't sung since I was in school. "Nobody knows the trouble I've seen. . . ."

That song strengthened me, and I understood we must all bear part of our pain in private. Nobody really grasps what another person goes through.

God, nobody else does understand. Only you. Help me to remember that we all have those times of feeling shut off from everyone else. In his own way, I wonder if he does too. Amen.

The little things

I had a busy life. I worked long hours, trying to get ahead, saving for retirement. She didn't complain about my not being around more. Yet I missed a lot of the little things in our life together. I'm aware of what I've missed because I've discovered some of them recently—for the first time.

We walk hand in hand in the moonlight and watch the fireflies. We laugh at the crunching of snow under our feet. We've gotten down on the floor with our year-old grandson and played with him. I look for little pleasures she can share with me. I'm thankful for the newness I discover in little things. That's when the little things truly mean a lot.

Creator God, thank you for the world of nature, the world of people, but most of all for the little things that provide us with daily pleasure. Amen.

Role changes

He was a good father to me but a little distant because he didn't know how to express feelings. He loved me and I knew it. He took care of me.

Now we've reversed roles. I'm the caregiver, and I'm beginning to feel like his father. I have to talk to him like one. "Dad, now it's time to come to the table," I say, or, "Let's take off your shoes now."

Sometimes he argues or gets difficult. If I try to hurry him he becomes confused. He looks like the same dad but he's different inside. I miss asking his advice and having him tell me stories about his childhood.

I like being Dad's primary caregiver. I think of it as my way to do something special for him. As if I can repay him for all the sacrifices he made for me.

God, thank you for Dad. I'm thankful that I can be here when he needs me. Amen.

Our strained marriage

I love my mother and I like doing things for her. Unfortunately, her sickness strains my marriage. The family tries to understand and wouldn't want me to lock her away somewhere.

I'd like to have Mother move in with us, but it wouldn't work. She's at her worst around my husband. She's snappish with the children, and they resent the special attention I show her.

Will her sickness eventually ruin my own marriage? How much do I owe my family and children? What can I stop doing for her that I can hire someone else to do? Hundreds of questions like this strike me every day. I'm not coping as well as I want to. I can't let out my frustrations around her. When I get home, I can't dump on my family. It's hard for me right now.

Loving God, you understand what I'm going through. Give me the strength and wisdom to do my best. Amen.

Talking eyes

When we first met, his eyes impressed me most. They were so alive and he communicated so much through them. During the years of our marriage I gradually stopped paying attention. Now his eyes are as important to me as they were when we first met.

I can't depend upon his words. Sometimes they're fairly normal. Other days he speaks in confused sentences or has spells of rambling. I watch his face, the way he stands or sits, but mostly his eyes.

It amazes me how much I have understood through the years without words. Often when I talk to him I think of myself as a detective trying to figure out his secret. Silly, perhaps, but it helps me to listen to his talking eyes and to hear his simplest gestures. It's not perfect, but it *is* communication.

God, you talk to us through nature, circumstances, and the world around us. It isn't so unusual to communicate without words, is it? Amen.

"I wish she'd die"

I hadn't meant to say those words, and deep remorse struck as soon as they came out. Yet they are true—at least part of the time. When she has a bad day or I'm on edge or tired, I think it would be easier for both of us if she died. It seems as if this illness will never end. It goes on and on.

I love her and don't want to let her go. I can't conceive of life without her. I finally talked with a friend whose wife had died the year before with Alzheimer's. He told me the feelings he had gone through. "You can't choose your feelings. You *can* choose your actions," he said.

God, just as my friend said, I can't do much about how I feel. Help me to do everything I can for her while I can. Thank you for loving her and for giving her to me for all these years. Amen.

FIVE

Self-Caring

Knowing us

I've learned a lot about myself as I've faced one crisis after another with Dad. As I've watched my own reactions, many of them surprised me. I'm more honest with myself and with family members.

I'm stronger for having gone through these past two years with Dad. I can do things I was sure I could never do before. Sometimes I can do them only because they have to be done.

I'm supposed to be the strong one—the one everybody depended on. Yet more than once I've gone to the others and said, "I'm worn out. I need a break. I can't handle any more."

I've learned that it's all right for me to get tired, be impatient, want time off. I've learned that my weaknesses and strengths are both part of me. I've learned to depend more on God. I often quote, "I can do everything through him who gives me strength" (Phil. 4:13, NIV).

God, you've always known me. Thank you for helping me know myself. Amen.

Family conference

The worst and the best in us came out during our family conference. We admitted deep-seated and long-hidden feelings against Mom.

In the end, though, we knew we had to pull together. Since then we've still had problems. One sister doesn't do all that I think she's supposed to do. I grumbled about it and my wife said, "But what would it be like if you were the only one Mom had?" Since then I've been less resentful and more honest about the amount of my own contribution. I've even wondered if the others think that sometimes I shirk my responsibility.

Right now we're all willing to help. We want to do what we can for Mom while we still have her with us. Despite all the resentment, failure, the love she didn't give us (and none of us ever gets enough), she is with us.

God, make us faithful in caring for Mom. Help us work together to make things smoother for one another. Amen.

The children too

We didn't know how to tell our children about their grandfather. They noticed that he acted odd at times. We finally explained. "Grandpa just doesn't remember things as well as you do. Something has gone wrong with his brain."

"Well, what do you think?" my husband asked our children.

"Kind of sad," our five-year-old said with tears in his eyes.

It surprised me that he understood at such a young age. I wondered why I had worried that the children might misunderstand or become fearful. Since then, they've accepted the severe phases of Dad's dementia more easily than we have. When I become exasperated, they remind me, "He can't help it. He can't remember how."

God, thank you for the simple wisdom of children. Thank you that they can teach us. Amen.

Burdening the children

If we had to do it all over again, I would involve the children earlier. At first I tried to protect them because I didn't want them worried or confused. The silence confused them more than an explanation, and once they understood they quickly volunteered to help. "She's our grandma."

Now and then they grow tired of the situation. Today I said, "Stay with Grandma while I run to the store."

"Do I have to?" our daughter asked. Our son stamped his foot when he had to help Grandma and couldn't go out to play.

We encourage the children to talk with us about how they feel. We're trying to equalize the load a little better. We know our children have become more compassionate toward other people because of Grandma's dementia.

God, thank you for our children and for the help they give us by sharing our load. Amen.

Self-care

If he asks me again, "When do we eat?" I think I'll scream. This is the fourth time in the last hour. Yet when it's finally time to sit down at the table, he won't eat. I cut up his food and feed him each spoonful. If I'm lucky he won't dribble too much. After I finished feeding him, I used to grab what I could to eat. I'd think that if I put in a TV dinner, it would be ready by the time I finished feeding him.

While we are careful to be sure our loved one gets a balanced meal, we may be neglecting our own nourishment. Unless we eat well, we will have neither the strength to care for the other nor the ability to experience the simple pleasure of a good meal. I finally admitted that we help no one by overlooking our own needs because of our caring for another.

Loving God, help me to understand that caring for my own needs isn't selfish. I wisely take care of me so that I can provide better care for my loved one. Amen.

Mini-vacations

I promised myself that I would always be able to take care of her no matter what. For a year I have done just that. Now I'm almost worn out. My ADRDA support group reminds me I'm human and can only handle so much.

"Pace yourself," one person said. "Only you know when you're doing too much." One member used to say to me, "Jesus said, 'Come apart and rest awhile.' Or come apart." I laughed at first but later I realized that if I didn't take care of me, who would be left to take care of her?

Now I treat myself to mini-vacations by having someone come in and stay with her. My time away may last half a day or only an hour. It's enough to renew my energy. That makes me a more effective caregiver.

God, thanks for the mini-vacations and for the renewing I receive. Amen.

From the outside

I didn't like having strangers come into the house to care for him. "He's my husband and I can do this," I insisted. Fortunately, the family and a few friends insisted more strongly. I hired someone to come in one afternoon and one evening a week.

For a while, I'd leave the house and worry about him all the time I was gone. I called two or three times just to check up on him.

Now that I've gotten used to having people from the outside, I enjoy my time away. Those free periods do wonders for me. During the rest of the week I plan how I'll spend my free time. It keeps me looking forward.

God, thank you for those who are willing to work among the demented. Bless their efforts because they bring so much help to people like me who need them. Amen.

Getting help

We always prided ourselves on being independent. I've never found it easy to ask others to help. Now I don't have much choice.

I can't do everything by myself. If I spend most of my time caring for her, I have little energy left to cook, clean, and do the miscellaneous other things we take for granted.

Recently we hired a maid to come every week. It confused her to have a stranger around so I arranged for the maid to come while she's at the senior day-care center. I go shopping with a neighbor each week while a family member stays with her.

I'm glad I finally asked for help. It makes everything easier for me, having someone from the outside.

God, you're always available to help, but I forget that you also help us through other people. Don't let me forget it again. Amen.

Friends

I've had a lot of friends over the years, and I tried to help them any way I could. "That's what friends are for," I used to say.

I never suspected I would ever need help myself. But I can't care for him all the time. He wears me out. So I call on my friends.

The first time I called on a church friend, I started apologizing and she interrupted me. "That's what friends are for," she said.

I laughed because I had to listen to my own little speech. I'm glad I did, too. Their help takes a load off me. But I'm grateful even more that these people care enough to help lift the load.

My best friend said, "At last I can do something important for you."

My heavenly Friend, thank you for the friends who care and who show it by all the practical things they do. Amen.

The centers

Three mornings a week—Monday, Wednesday, and Friday—a van pulls up in front of our house and takes her to the senior citizens' center. On those days she's sufficiently tired by nightfall to sleep well. She's used to the familiar trip, and I think she even looks forward to going.

At first I didn't think it would work out. She had tears in her eyes as she pleaded with me. "Don't send me away. Don't get rid of me."

The people at the center had warned me to expect something like that. So I went to the center with her in the van for two weeks. Once I was sure she knew the routine, I let her go alone. She didn't want to get into the van without me, but I said, "It's fine, dear. You'll have a good ride and a nice lunch."

The senior citizens' center provides a warm atmosphere and she's around other people. I'm glad for such places.

God, thank you for those who understand the needs of people like us. Amen.

Programs, programs!

I heard about programs sponsored by the federal government, our county, our city, churches, and synagogues. People frequently said, "Have you thought about . . . ?"

It took me a long time to do anything because I didn't want to depend on agencies and organizations. They sounded so impersonal. Who could give him the kind of care I could provide at home?

"These programs have come about because people care," the social worker said. "We're aware of your situation. These efforts are our way of responding to your need."

The programs have some restrictions such as age, physical condition, income, and type of help they offer. I have found that Meals on Wheels takes care of our big meals. A federal program provides physical exercise and day-care service during the week. We're both a lot better off because of these programs.

God, often your help is available and we don't ask. Forgive us for being stubborn and proud. Amen.

Enjoying life

She still likes to sing the familiar songs, mostly hymns and patriotic anthems. One day she made me play "God Bless America" on the piano over and over. As my fingers moved across the keyboard it occurred to me how little it actually took for her to enjoy life.

She has three good friends who visit every week. They don't say much—and they don't need to. Just their presence gives her a lift.

We used to like to gaze at the stars or walk under a full moon. We've started doing that again. Or we sit and stare at the glowing sunset. One morning she watched contentedly for more than an hour while two chipmunks ran up and down our oak tree.

I'm enjoying life more as I appreciate again these simple things we have around us all the time.

God of joy, thank you for giving us a world of beauty that we can find pleasure in. Amen.

My illness

Until recently, my health remained reasonably good. Now I'm facing surgery, and I have nagging worries about what will happen if I die or become unable to care for him. Who will do it? How will he react with someone else around?

I've talked with the rest of the family, and we've decided to have them stay here in shifts until I'm home again. Moving him from the house would probably upset him.

I'm trying to remember everything the family needs to know about our routine. I want to do as much as I can before I go to the hospital. I don't want to lie there and worry about him all the time.

God, my husband remains constantly in my thoughts. Help me trust you to care for him as I know you care for me. Amen.

In case I die

I tried to protect the family from knowing about my physical condition. After all, having a mother with a dementing illness causes enough pressure. Then I decided it would be unfair to them if something happened to me without warning.

It took me a couple of weeks to do anything, but I'm glad I finally did. I updated my will. I explained to the children about my condition. I tried to give them as much information as possible.

"Dad, don't talk this way," my older daughter said. It hurt her to hear me speak about the possibility of my dying. "In case I die," I said, "you'd be under enough of a shock; you won't need more pressure. Let's take care of it now— just in case."

God, I am acutely aware that life is a gift from you. I don't know how long I'll have this gift. Give me wisdom in planning for her as I make plans for myself. Amen.

A new pride

He has always done so much for me. If anything needed fixing in the house, he did it. He took care of our finances and paid the bills.

He can't do any of those things now. They have fallen into my lap. The first realization of it scared me. *I can't possibly do it without his help.* Yet I've learned that I can.

I took driving lessons. I had to go back three times before I passed the road test, but I have a license. I keep up the house by myself. I had to call the plumbers once and the air-conditioning people last summer. But I can do it!

The house isn't as neat as it used to be. I haven't done anything outside except cut the grass. But I have gained a new confidence in myself. It's a new pride, a new faith in what I can do because I have to do it.

God, thanks for making me equal to the tasks you've given me. But then, that's always been your way, hasn't it? Amen.

SIX

Advancing Stages

She doesn't know me

Mom's brother from out of state visited. They chatted a few minutes before she asked, "Who are you?"

"I'm your brother. I'm Tom."

"I don't know you," she insisted.

We told him not to argue but smile, keep his voice calm, and say again, "I'm your brother, Tom."

Mom has a condition known as *agnosia*, where the brain doesn't work right, and she often doesn't recognize people, even family members. We accept it as part of her sickness that we have to live with. She didn't reject Uncle Tom or me or anyone. We believe she still knows all of us, but her confused brain can't put all the information together.

Her not knowing us is an inaccurate term. More correctly, she doesn't *recognize* us. Lack of recognition is not the same as rejection.

God, you always know us—and knowing us means caring for us. Remind us of that often. Amen.

What did you say?

This morning I listened to the robins in our backyard. I called my husband so he could enjoy it with me. Then I remembered: he can't hear them.

I don't know when his hearing started going bad. He turned up the TV volume. He accused me of mumbling. When visitors came, he couldn't hear their words and thought they talked about him.

His impaired hearing along with his increased dementia makes it harder to communicate. I have learned, however, to stand where he sees my face when I speak. I gesture to explain my meaning. At other times, I guide his hand or gently pull him.

While we have learned ways to compensate for his increasing world of silence, nothing ever takes the place of his own ability to hear for himself.

All-hearing God, speak to him in the quietness of his heart so that he can still know your voice that gives him peace. Amen.

"It's not my home"

We moved so we could live closer to our son and his family. For the first week I wondered if I had made a mistake. "I don't live here," she said over and over. "This is not my home."

Even though I told her every day that we had moved, she kept forgetting. Each time it reminded me of her dementia. I learned that when she insisted she didn't live here, the best thing was for me to say quietly, "Dear, we live here now. This is our house."

It took two weeks for her to accept her new surroundings.

God, new things and new places are often hard on us. It's been especially difficult for her to adjust. Keep assuring her that everything is all right. Help her know she is secure in your hand. Amen.

Messy eating

He was always a fastidious person. It hurt to watch him cause a mess at the table. I've accepted that and learned ways to make mealtime easier and more pleasant for both of us.

I let him use his fingers or a soupspoon for most of his food. A plastic tablecloth makes it easier to wipe up the inevitable spills. He gets his food in a plastic bowl because it's easier for him. I don't have to worry about breakage if he drops it.

When I tried several kinds of food in his bowl at the same time, the variety confused him. He didn't seem to know which to eat first. Now I give him one item at a time.

He always sprinkled liberal amounts of ketchup on his food. Now I do the seasoning for him because he does not seem to grasp how much to put on.

God, as I learn to feed his body, feed my mind with wisdom in caring for him. Amen.

Spoon-feeding

I used to like to watch her eat with her graceful motions and dainty bites. Now she can't even feed herself because her hand and her brain don't seem to work together.

I give her small bites, sometimes reminding her to chew. Occasionally I have to say, "All right, dear, swallow it." Most of the time the eating is pleasant because I've accepted the situation as it is. I've discovered that when I'm cheerful it seems to make her more cooperative.

One day when it depressed me to feed her, I thought about God and humanity. No matter how old we are, learning lessons must be like God spoon-feeding us. God offers us a small amount of understanding at a time and then waits for us to absorb it before we are ready for new insight.

God of wisdom and knowledge, as you continue to spoon-feed me with understanding, help me to feed and care lovingly for her. Amen.

Medicine time

"I took my pills this morning."

"Why do I have to take all of this stuff?"

"Tastes terrible. I don't want that junk."

He often refuses medication. At first I tried to reason with him and, failing that, insisted. Neither worked. Now I act as if I assume he will take the medicine. I say, "Here, dear, Dr. Brown wants you to take these two pills." I place a glass of orange juice to his mouth. "That's fine. Just swallow." It usually works.

I love him and want to do anything to help him stay active and healthy as long as possible. Sometimes it's hard, but I know it's the right thing to do.

Wise and loving God, I'm reminded that sometimes we fight and revolt against what's best for us. You don't give up on us. Help me not to give up on him. Amen.

The little pains

She can't tell me when she hurts, even though she talks fluently. I watch for any signs she's not well.

Fortunately we have a good doctor who doesn't lightly dismiss her. He checks her carefully. For example, when she had the flu, she ran a fever and her eyes had what I called a sick look. The doctor diagnosed her and I put her to bed when we got back home. It took a week before she got over the flu.

When she lay in bed and I knew she was sick, I kept wishing I could take the pain away from her or feel the pain myself instead. It hurt me to see her suffer. But then, maybe that's the way it is when two people love each other—they find it hard to bear up when their mates are in pain.

Compassionate God, you feel my pain and give me strength to keep on. You feel hers as well. Thank you for caring about us. Amen.

Other kinds of pain

The literature assures me that Alzheimer's disease causes no pain. Lately I've been thinking about other kinds of pain he must be going through. The pain of not understanding the world he lives in. The pain of confusion when he doesn't recognize a face or a voice. When he temporarily forgets how to tie his shoe or button his shirt.

He suffers in silence because he can't express how he feels. He has lost the ability to play games like Scrabble, something he enjoyed immensely.

I feel pain too. I have to watch the irreversible changes going on. I shed my tears in private so that he doesn't see. Once in a while I find myself asking, "How long, God? How long must it go on?"

Faithful God, you never answer that question, but you do give me the strength to cope with each day's trials. I am thankful. Amen.

Pressure sores

Because she sat still a lot, she developed pressure sores—decubitus ulcers—particularly on her hips and shoulder blades.

When I urged her, "Dear, get up and move," she argued with me.

"I'm fine the way I am," she'd say, or just, "No."

I'm finding ways to get her moving around more. I've made a little game of it by keeping count of the number of times I can get her out of the chair in a day. I call her to help set the table, to put away the silverware. I try to get her interested in looking out the window. As she sits in her chair, hours at a time, unaware she needs to move her body, I remind myself that we humans are like that. We don't know what we really need. We ask for all kinds of things but we *need* few of them.

God, give me what I need to give her proper care, such as love, strength, wisdom, and peace. Amen.

Losing

Dad lost his glasses and accused me of stealing them. This happens three or four times a week.

One day we had a visitor and he lost his wallet. "You stole my money!" he screamed at the man. The words confused the visitor. Dad sounded and acted normal otherwise. Once we explained the situation, our friend understood.

Dad will probably continue to lose things and jump to confused ideas that one of us stole them. We've found the simple way to respond is to say, "I'll help you look for it."

No one likes to lose anything. Losing a special object like his glasses must be like losing a bit of himself. I wonder if it doesn't frighten him.

God, none of us likes to lose anything. Make us patient as we understand the great losses he is going through. Amen.

Embarrassing moments

She embarrassed me almost every time I took her out in public. If she were not sick, that's one of the last things she would do.

Once she said to a waitress, "Your uniform sure is dirty." When an old friend visited, she pointed to me. "He's keeping me a prisoner. He wants all my money." I have learned to say quietly, "She has Alzheimer's. Please forgive her."

As public awareness of Alzheimer's increases, people are more understanding. I no longer feel discomforted. I accept her as she is, not how she ought to be or used to be. She doesn't intentionally try to embarrass, and since she's not disconcerted, I am less sensitive to other people's responses.

God, help me remember that she's only behaving normally for her. Help me always to accept and to love her as she is. Amen.

He doesn't understand

He sat absorbed in front of the TV. I said, "Dear, I'm going to the bedroom. I'll be right back. Do you understand?" He nodded. I had hardly gotten out of the room before he started calling my name. Once I reappeared he turned around and watched TV again. I realized then that he *didn't* understand.

I can't take it for granted that he understands simply because he says he does.

At first it troubled me because he didn't grasp the meaning of my words. I rushed out of the room crying. Now I've learned to say, "You don't understand." I tell him again. Occasionally he never grasps it, and I give up. Usually, if I work patiently he figures out what I'm trying to say. I find great comfort in even those small victories.

God, he doesn't understand a lot of what I mean. Help him to know that I love him and that I'm with him just as you love us and are with us. Amen.

Private indignity

She is incontinent. I think it ripped away a little more of her dignity when we faced the reality that she wets herself without warning.

She cried once, "I didn't mean to."

I think of these accidents as just that—accidents. She doesn't intend to urinate on herself. She gets no pleasure from the indignity.

Yet when it happens three or four times daily, I find myself resentful of having to help her take care of her private functions.

We take as many precautions as we can. I lead her to the bathroom within half an hour after she drinks anything. That helps but it's no cure.

The real battle for me has been in accepting this as just one more thing over which she has no control.

All-powerful God, you help us when we can't do things for ourselves. Help me to do the same for her. Amen.

The invisible person

I don't know where it began or who started it, but one day I realized that visitors treated Dad like an invisible person. They asked me or one of the family, "How's your father doing today?"

"He's better today," we'd answer, or "He's not doing too well."

All the time Dad sat in the same room with us and nobody asked *him*.

Dad's memory is impaired. He's going downhill. He has developed a few peculiarities but he's still alive. He's human. Above all, he has feelings.

Yesterday when a friend asked me a question about him, I turned to Dad and said, "She wants to know how you're feeling today."

"A little tired but all right," he said.

I've determined that no one will look upon Dad as an invisible person. He's present, and we want him to know that we're not ignoring him.

God, help us remain aware of Dad as a visible person with feelings. Amen.

Striking out

Mother hit me. She isn't strong enough to hurt me physically. But, along with the verbal tirade, I reacted badly. I yelled back and she got worse.

Mother wasn't angry at me even though she shouted when she struck me. She gets that way when the TV gets loud, a lot of action takes place, or when several people come into the room. Even if she used to know them, they are strangers now and their presence confuses her.

We think it frightens her to see a room full of "strangers." We now limit the number of visitors at any one time.

Mother's condition makes me look at myself. When things go wrong or events take place over which I have no control, I tend to strike out. I react differently, but the principle is the same.

God, make me more sympathetic of Mom's situation and make me an instrument of your peace in her life. Amen.

Insults and profanity

We needed time away from the house and from Dad. We hired a neighbor to stay with him for three hours.

When we returned she was crying because he had said, "You're too fat, you stupid bitch. You're not married, are you? You're too ugly for any man." He followed up with a string of profanity.

We explained his condition and she felt better. Since then, we warn anyone *in advance* what might happen. We've found it helpful to ask the person to come early while we're still home and let Dad get used to having a stranger around.

I don't know why Dad talks that way—he never did it before his illness. That's one of his symptoms. We accept it and overlook it because we accept Dad.

Understanding God, help me to be sensitive to Dad and to love him in his confused state. Amen.

Catastrophic reactions

I hated it when we had to go someplace. Getting her meal, dressing, and bathing her became an ordeal because she refused help and stubbornly thwarted me.

I was forcing her to remember too many things at one time. She reacted by refusing to do anything. Experts call it *catastrophic reaction* and it doesn't mean obstinacy. Now I try to think everything through in advance that she must do. But I tell her the next step only after she's completed the previous one. I say, "Now I'm going to wash your face. Feel the soap on the cloth," and let her touch it. "I'm going to rinse your face now. Feel the warm water."

This avoids the confusion and difficulty we had in the past. When we complete a total task such as bathing, I pause and kiss her or hold her for a minute and say, "That's fine. You did that well."

Caregiving God, when I consider your patient understanding for me, it helps me to be more understanding of her. Amen.

Apraxia

When did I notice that he shuffled? That he listed slightly to the left? I do remember the first time I heard that dreaded word *apraxia*.

Looking back, I could see apraxia in many ways. Maybe I didn't want to see it before. His handwriting had become shaky and he avoided signing his name. He had trouble holding a glass when he wanted a drink. I kept telling myself, He won't get worse. Yet he did.

When I start to feel sorry for myself, I think how he must be feeling over his deteriorating condition. When I grow weary of caregiving, I think of our marriage vows: "for better for worse, . . . in sickness and in health." That vow is as valid today as it was then.

God of the universe, no matter what our condition in life you promised to be with us and you are. That gives us peace and renews our courage. Thank you. Amen.

Repeating, repeating

She washed dishes, not once but again and again and again. Sometimes she picked up clean dishes and washed them. It kept her occupied, and I made sure she did nothing to hurt herself.

I had heard about people who "get stuck" in an action, as though they can't stop repeating it.

Since then I've done things that distract her attention, and it works. Most of the time I hand her one dish at a time and say, "Please put this away." Or I let her hold a dish and we put it away together. I like to think this gives her a sense of being helpful. I sometimes wonder if she feels useless and unneeded. If so, perhaps this helps her.

God, we all need to be needed by someone. Thank you for letting me be used to help her. I grumble about it sometimes and I get tired, too. But I'm glad I can be here when she needs me. Amen.

Following me

Today I wanted to run out into the street and scream, Stop following me! Sit down and leave me alone!

Sometimes I resent his following me around all day. I want to push him away or tie him down. I can't even go to the bathroom unless I leave the door open for him to see me.

I have a few friends who come to the house, and they talk to him, take him for a ride, or occupy him so that I can leave. Then I'm better for several days. I'm learning to accept this behavior as typical of those with dementia. I say aloud to myself, "You're the most important person in his life. He's afraid you'll leave him. He needs you here. He feels lost and confused."

I'm the only security he has. He needs me.

God, sometimes I feel lost and alone—just like he does. Thanks for helping me to understand his condition better. Amen.

Complaints and accusations

"You hate me!" she said. "You hate me!" The words shocked me. How could she think such a thing? What had I done to merit that kind of charge? It also hurt—hurt deeply—for her to accuse me like that.

Once she said to a salesman, "He's trying to kill me so he can collect the insurance." She's made other outrageous statements like that since then.

I now understand her a little better, although it still hurts. Intellectually I know she's unaware of what's going on. She may be saying that she's frightened, that she's afraid to die, that she feels unloved. I try to understand and not let it bother me. Most of the time it doesn't. Just once in a while it gets to me. But I'm learning . . . slowly.

Wise God, I don't know what's going on inside of her and she doesn't either. But help both of us in this painful situation and give us your peace. Amen.

Wandering

He wandered off three times before I accepted it as a problem. The first time he strayed while we were in the grocery store. The second time in a department store. One day he opened the front door and went out—I didn't hear him leave. A neighbor two doors away saw him and phoned.

I don't know why he wanders. The experts offer many reasons. I'm not concerned about *why* as much as I want to prevent it from happening.

I've done two things to help in case he does it again. He wears a Medic Alert bracelet saying "Memory Impaired." In his wallet he carries a card with his name, phone number, and the same words. I worry about his getting lost. What if he gets hurt by walking in front of traffic? Or just wandering in confusion?

God, I know you are his shepherd and you're always with your sheep. I need help so that I can rest in the secure knowledge of your shepherding care over him. Amen.

Demands

"I want my dinner." Mother's words came out in a tone of voice that said *now!* It didn't matter that she had eaten only minutes before or that on another occasion she had demanded dinner only ten minutes earlier. When she started that call for dinner (or other demands throughout the day), only minutes lapsed before she said it again. "Dinner will be ready soon," I tell her, or else, "You ate a few minutes ago. But I'll get you something else before you go to bed."

One Monday she started demanding that we call the doctor about her appointment. "Mother, your appointment with Dr. Morgan is on Friday. Today is Monday." That temporarily satisfied her.

Because of her memory loss she asked again a few minutes later. I made myself answer as calmly as the first time. She didn't recall asking me.

God, I keep asking you to be with us. You are, but I forget too often. Forgive me. Amen.

Night trips

He has started getting up occasionally at night and wandering about the house. I've tried to keep him busy during the day so that he's tired enough to sleep at night.

He gets out of bed and dresses. He walks around in the darkened house. The first time I woke up and yelled, "What are you doing? Go back to sleep!"

Almost as quickly as I said the words I felt bad because it further confused him. Psalm 139 comforts me as I watch my husband wander around in the house in the middle of the night. It reminds me of God's being with us no matter where we are or what we're doing.

"If I say, 'Let only darkness cover me, and the light about me be night,' even the darkness is not dark to thee, for the night is bright as the day; for darkness is as light with thee" (Ps. 139:11–12).

All-seeing God, whether darkness or light, you are with us, reminding us of your love. Remind us often, God, because we're easily confused. Amen.

Safekeeping

When we were kids I remember Mom used to store things in her bedroom closet she didn't want us to find. It was the one place in the house we never went into unless she instructed us.

She must have some kind of memory of putting things away in a safe place. Yet she no longer remembers hiding things. For instance, I found the iron tucked behind a box. Her favorite hand mirror and hairbrush disappeared one day and, sure enough, she had hidden them in a safe place.

I try to understand this behavior, even when I get impatient at times because I can't find the eggbeater or a mixing bowl.

When I begin to feel exasperated, I comfort myself by saying aloud, "Mom now lives in a strange world. She seeks protection and safety in her own way. It's all right."

God, we all need a sense of safety, don't we? Keep assuring me that I'm safe in your protective care. Amen.

Hiding things

He's been hiding things for the past two months. I missed a cereal bowl. A few days later a second one disappeared. Then spoons. One day he took the toaster.

"Dear, do you know what happened to the can opener?" I asked.

"I didn't take it," he said.

I shouldn't have asked, but it was a perfectly natural reaction. I didn't say anything more and later found the can opener under the bed. He didn't remember doing it.

Now I put most things out of sight as much as possible. I also know his favorite hiding places. I've accepted this as one of my own adjustments.

God of life, it comforts me to know we can't hide anything from you. And you never stop loving us either. Thanks, God. Amen.

Sexual behavior

Recently she started to scratch herself in the genital area. She pulled off her underpants and threw them in the wastebasket.

My first reaction was to snap at her and tell her not to do such things. Immediately I thought of her exposing herself in public or behaving inappropriately. I forced myself to be calm and helped her put her underwear back on. I go on the assumption she's lost her social sensibility and the underpants felt uncomfortable.

I wonder if God doesn't smile at my confusion. I thought of times in my life when I failed God through inappropriate behavior or downright disobedience. My actions didn't embarrass God. God knows that's the way we humans are.

Heavenly Father, thank you for understanding me and the muddles and confusions in my life. Help me to understand her, especially at this time in her life. Amen.

SEVEN

Later Decisions

Jerking movements

We were sitting and watching the sun go down when his left leg jerked rapidly. He seemed unaware of it. It scared me and I phoned the doctor.

He gave me the fancy name for it—myoclonus jerks. It helped to know it wasn't a seizure or would lead to one. He added, "We have no treatments for this." As I watched another jerking movement, I thought of a story in the Bible. Jesus told Peter that when he was young, he went wherever he chose. When he grew old, another person would take him where he didn't want to go (see John 21:18–19).

Jesus referred to Peter's death, but it made me think that my husband is now at the stage of life where he can't choose where to go and has little control over his own body. One more thing to remind me that he and I are mortal after all.

God, you guide our lives; we are in your hands. You are holding our hands, leading us onward. Thank you. Amen.

Nervousness

Mom started walking through the house, wringing her hands and shaking her head. We tried to find out what was upsetting her. She didn't know and couldn't seem to stop.

We tried to reason with her but that didn't work. Then we grasped that Mom perceived the mood in the household. We were discussing her ultimate care. How long could we continue to care for her? Should we place her in a nursing home?

We think she picked up the mood even though she didn't understand the conversation. The discussion upset our whole family. We also felt we were failing her. She can feel it when things aren't right even though she doesn't seem to know what they are. We've been careful to discuss emotional issues away from her, and she has not been noticeably upset since.

God, help us provide a loving atmosphere for Mom. Teach us more about peace and let it show in our home. Amen.

Prolonging

He's going to die. I've known that for a long time. I suspect he knows it too. "Is it right to let him go on like this?" I asked our minister. I asked our doctor. No one gave me an answer that satisfied.

I don't know what kind of answer I want. I hear of cases where a husband killed his terminally ill wife or a child did it to a parent. "I couldn't stand to see him suffer," they said.

I've thought of doing something to bring about his death, yet I know I couldn't do it. I don't want him to die and I don't want him to go on half living.

It's helped to talk to others who have these same feelings. When I pray I ask God to help him and me to bear up under the strain. Sometimes I want God to take him, and other days I plead, "Let him live a little longer."

God, bring peace to my troubled heart. Help me to accept life as it is and to accept your strength at the same time. Amen.

Alone together

Despite our years together, we haven't been happy. Although we stayed together and never discussed divorce, now I am alone. I don't love her, at least not the way I did at the beginning. If we had established a closeness, it might make it easier now that she's sick. But I wonder. If we had been really close, the change might be harder to bear.

I don't want to neglect her, and I do as much as I can. I also know that I can't pour everything into caring for her and have nothing for myself.

I've decided to put her in a nursing home. I want to be as dutiful as I can, and I don't want to feel guilty later for neglecting her. Yet I am alive and I'll probably live for years after she's gone. I'm trying to make a new beginning for myself: a life of being alone.

God, am I selfish? I don't want to be. I want to do everything I can for her, and I rely on your strength. Amen.

Will it ever end?

He's been sick a long time. I try not to count days, but I do. I try not to think about next month or next year. But I do. Sometimes I reach the end of my patience. I want to scream, "Will this never end? How long does it have to go on?"

I feel trapped inside this house. I have no freedom. I can't make plans. I can't relax. I'm tired. If I worked for a company, I'd have resigned already. I can't resign. I can't walk out. At best I can get away a few hours at a time. I have a few special people who help make my load a little easier.

His sickness *will* end someday. A part of me wants that to happen soon. Another part of me cries out, Not yet, not yet! My days fluctuate between the two moods.

God, help me to understand that it's all right to want it to end and yet to hold on to him. Amen.

When she dies

She's going to die. The doctor says the immediate cause won't be Alzheimer's. She said they usually die from pneumonia or malnutrition (from refusal to eat). I'm not concerned about the final cause of death. I'm more concerned about preparing myself. Then I feel guilty. *Why do I keep thinking about myself when she's the one who's suffering?*

I must keep on living. When she dies I'll still be here. I'll have to adjust to a world without the most important person in my life.

When I can look at it like that, I know I must plan ahead. I'm preparing myself to face her death and go on alone. That thought hurts and scares me.

God, my friend and companion in life, we've been together a long time, you and I. She's been part of my life for a long time too. As you prepare her to leave, make me ready to stay and to want to keep on living without her. Amen.

At home? At the hospital?

I have choices. I can keep him at home until the end or send him to the hospital. I've investigated hospice programs. I don't know what to do. I keep thinking that maybe when he dies, it will happen in a way that the choice will be taken from me.

Am I morbid to think about such things? Does it show lack of feeling? I know I'm tired and I can't remember when I wasn't worn out. I also know it has to end someday and in some place.

Right now I'm trying to decide if I have the strength to give him the care he needs as he gets worse. I want to be strong enough to handle anything. But can I? Our deaths are in God's hands just as much as our lives have been.

Powerful God, give me peace as he and I get closer to the end of the road together. Whether the end comes at home or in some kind of hospital, I know you'll be with him and with me as you have been with us all our lives. Amen.

Making choices

Before I made the decision to move her to a nursing home, we talked about it—every day for three weeks. She cried the first few times.

I kept at it. Once I had decided and told her, she refused to go. She accused me of wanting to get rid of her. I didn't argue, only assured her of my love. After that, each decision I faced, I asked, What choices can I give her? I knew the more she participated in the planning, the easier the adjustment. I said, "You're going to Happy View soon, dear. I'd like you to help me pick out the clothes you want to take."

I consulted her on skirts, shoes, coats, hats— anything that gave her a choice. It took many attempts before she said, "Don't send that striped blue skirt. Doesn't fit right." She was reconciled.

God, thank you for giving us choices in life. Help me to remember she still needs to have choices too. Amen.

Going it alone

I'm not a woman who cries easily. But last Thursday I cried most of the day. I took my husband to a nursing home and left him.

I had been fighting this decision for months. I finally had to do it. I'm thankful that our daughter who lives in another city insisted on it. "Mom, he's too much for you. You can't take care of him *and* yourself any longer."

She was right, but it still hurt. I felt as if I had betrayed him. I felt like a failure because I "put him away." I worry about his getting enough to eat, receiving proper medication.

Yet I made the right decision. I'm trying to accept it when I walk through the empty house or get into an empty bed. But I still hurt. Tears still come often.

Loving Father and Friend, ease my pain as I adjust to life alone. Help him to adjust to his new situation. Amen.

The new residence

I tried to take care of her on my own and eventually I couldn't manage it. We hired help, but between the cost and the inability to keep anyone, we gave that up. Church people and civic friends volunteered their help. That eased the strain somewhat. Yet I couldn't ask them to keep coming. I had to put her in a place where she could get the care she needs. I know that with a dementing illness the patient must have familiarity. In the new place, I stayed with her throughout the entire day for two weeks. I tried to make her room as much like home as possible.

I painfully reminded myself, This is her new residence. She lives here. She no longer lives with me. This is now her home.

God of heaven and earth, we become so attached to things and places. Help her to become familiar with her new home as she awaits her final home. Amen.

Adjusting

I hoped for an easy adjustment. It hurt to watch him cry. I felt guilty when he pleaded, "Take me home." Many days I left the nursing home praying for a way to take him home again.

To make it easier for him, I spent a lot of time there. I still stay all afternoon—usually his best time. He's accepting it slowly. He doesn't beg me to take him home anymore. Many days he doesn't even know he's not at home. Some days I'm not sure which hurts worse—his being there or his not knowing where he is.

At first I thought only about his getting used to the changes. I had to make adjustments too. With all my supportive friends, it has still not been easy. My own difficulties make me more patient with his adjustment.

Patient God, I'm still learning that some things take time, like adjusting to a new lifestyle. Help us—both of us—to adjust. Amen.